A YEAR OF
Self-Care
JOURNAL

52 WEEKS
TO CULTIVATE POSITIVITY AND JOY

Allison Task, MS, PCC

**ROCKRIDGE
PRESS**

For Clementine Task, who has taken outstanding care of herself since she was born. May it continue all of your days.

For general information on our other products and services or to obtain technical support, please contact our Customer Care Department within the United States at (866) 744-2665, or outside the United States at (510) 253-0500.

Rockridge Press publishes its books in a variety of electronic and print formats. Some content that appears in print may not be available in electronic books, and vice versa.

TRADEMARKS: Rockridge Press and the Rockridge Press logo are trademarks or registered trademarks of Callisto Media Inc. and/or its affiliates, in the United States and other countries, and may not be used without written permission. All other trademarks are the property of their respective owners. Rockridge Press is not associated with any product or vendor mentioned in this book.

Cover Designer: Emma Hall
Interior Designer: Jill Lee
Art Producer: Sara Feinstein
Editor: Jesse Aylen
Production Editor: Emily Sheehan
Production Manager: Holly Haydash

Author photo: Donna Dotan

ISBN: Print 978-1-64876-421-9

R0

"We delight in the beauty of a butterfly but rarely admit the changes it has gone through to achieve that beauty."
—Maya Angelou

Contents

Introduction

Welcome to your *A Year of Self-Care Journal*. By following the guidance within these pages, and releasing inspiration within yourself, you may find yourself in a very different place in one year's time.

I congratulate you (and please congratulate yourself!) for taking this important action that will bring a greater sense of well-being, joy, and contentment both to the life you have now and to the life you will create.

My name is Allison Task. I have been working as a life coach for almost 20 years (before coaching was a "thing"). Prior to my work as a coach, I wrote cookbooks and hosted television and internet shows about food. And in the nineties, I was one of those kids trying to convince corporate executives that some day we would all be shopping on the internet.

Today, I run a private coaching practice where I work with clients who are transitioning from one phase of life to another and are interested in finding greater meaning and purpose in their lives. I am the mother of four children, and I have a dog and some fish. I am married to a man who is my partner in life, work, and raising our family. I go to sleep early and wake before the sun rises on most days. I live a simple life. I love my family and my work, and I consider it an honor to help clients create lives that they love too.

Self-care is the essence of my work. It is an act of self-care to identify and pursue the kind of work that makes use of the abundant skills and talents you were born with and have developed over a lifetime. It is an act of self-care to prioritize your health and to nurture and grow fulfilling relationships.

Self-care is knowing yourself, and providing yourself with a life that fills your cup, repairs, and replenishes you. It is also pushing yourself to take on challenges in order to grow. It's more than just taking it easy. There is a deliberate tension between repair and growth, taking on a challenge that means moving from stasis and returning to it. Self-care involves taking on that challenge, then recognizing and celebrating your growth.

I've spent the better part of my career facilitating wellness for my clients, supporting them as they take control of their physical, mental, spiritual, emotional, and social health. I practice what I preach: I take my self-care seriously. I take on new challenges constantly, learning and growing. I rest. I repair.

I walk the walk before I talk it (or write it), so every action I ask you to take in these pages is an action my clients and I have also taken. In fact, these exercises are the "best of" list—the classics, client favorites—vetted, tested, and approved.

In each week of this journal, you will find an affirmation or inspiring quote, a writing prompt, a self-care goal, and a self-care exercise that provides opportunities for you to engage in physical, mental, spiritual, emotional, and social self-care.

These pages are designed to help you engage in deeper thoughts and take tangible actions that promote self-care. Although some exercises may resonate with you better than others, I ask that you give them—and yourself—a chance. You never know which will become your new go-to. By year's end, you'll find yourself with a self-care tool kit and some self-care habits that have become part of your life.

Thank you, and your future well-cared-for self, for beginning this journey and for trusting me as your guide. I look forward to a productive and transformative year together.

THE BASICS OF SELF-CARE

The umbrella of self-care is wide, and it includes the essentials we've likely heard about since we were kids: getting a good night's sleep, providing your body with adequate exercise, and eating healthy foods.

It's also so much more. It includes creating and fostering positive relationships, engaging with your community, helping others, and accepting help when it's offered.

Self-care refers to taking responsibility for your health and wellness, empowering yourself to be the expert on you. According to the World Health Organization (WHO), self-care is a global necessity, and it encompasses a wide range of principles, as stated on the WHO website:

The fundamental principles of self-care include: aspects of the individual (e.g., self-reliance, empowerment, autonomy, personal responsibility, self-efficacy) as well as the greater community (e.g., community participation, community involvement, community empowerment).

Self-care starts with your relationship with yourself and radiates outward. It involves slowing down to listen to yourself and ensuring that your needs are met. Far from being a selfish act, as a cared-for person, you are able to better engage with the world and help satisfy the needs of the community, which is also beneficial for you—a self-care boomerang.

In the pages of this journal, I've identified five key areas: physical, mental, spiritual, emotional, and social. Each week, I will feature one key area and give you a specific self-care goal to work toward. Along the way, I provide an inspirational quote or affirmation, as well as writing prompts and exercises that will encourage you to reflect, then take tangible action in these areas.

In the 1950s, self-care was a concept that doctors used to empower people with special needs to take responsibility for their own health. In the '70s and '80s, the Black poet and activist Audre Lorde used the term to describe the self-care she engaged in to face her cancer battles. "Caring for myself is not self-indulgence. It is self-preservation, and that is an act of political warfare," Lorde wrote in *A Burst of Light and Other Essays*.

Since then, self-care has become a billion-dollar industry, selling wine, bubble bath, and baubles. *Let's reclaim it from the world of consumerist noise and return it to its rightful place as a tool for self-empowerment and self-efficacy.* You can be the expert on you. You are in the best position to listen to yourself and advocate for your own needs.

Self-care has two components: growth and replenishment. We were not built to be in a state of stasis; we were built for dynamism. By providing yourself with the opportunity to try new things, you will grow.

Self-care is taking the initiative to go out into the world, grow, learn, participate, and contribute. It's stretching before *and after* exercise; it is exercise itself. It's taking note of your health and taking responsibility for your wellness. It's applauding your own accomplishments. By putting forth effort, then resting and repairing, you will build a stronger you. From there, you radiate wellness out into the world and help others and the world, serving as a beacon of joy, contentment, and light, which is fulfilling as well.

Ambitious? Sure. That's where self-care can take you. Let's make this life, this month, this day, this moment, the best it can be. And then we can look back, celebrate the moment, and get a good night's sleep.

That's self-care.

TYPE: Emotional

We don't laugh because we're happy, we are happy because we laugh.

—WILLIAM JAMES

Goal: Laugh. Put yourself in situations where you can laugh, giggle, lose control, experience happiness, and feel unfettered joy. Recognize that you can intentionally seek pleasure and find it!

When was the last time you had a big belly laugh? One of those *I'm-laughing-so-hard-I'm-crying* laughs? Take a few minutes to recall what made you laugh, who you were with, and how it felt.

This week, enjoy some comedy. Whether it's going to a comedy club, playing a game, reading the comics, or watching your favorite stand-up comic or rom-coms, indulge yourself in whatever is funny to you. Ask your friends and families for recommendations, or crowdsource some ideas. See if you can let yourself laugh so hard you end up in tears. Try to spend 2 to 5 hours this week engaging with content that makes you laugh.

WEEK 2

All my feelings are welcome. Like flowers at a flower shop, I can choose from a wide variety of feelings, each beautiful in its own way. And when I have a physical response, I can explore the sensation by associating it with an emotion.

Goal: Develop an emotional vocabulary so that you can more specifically identify and feel emotions. Add more emotions to your list and practice using them.

How are you feeling right now? Take a few minutes to identify how you feel and where you feel it, physically and emotionally. Say five to ten words out loud that describe your emotions, then write them down.

Continued >

Emotions are like crayons: Sometimes we keep using the same ones over and over again, and sometimes we use a broader range of options. With those, we can color our lives with more nuance. In the 1970s, researchers identified six basic universal emotions, but by 2017, Dacher Keltner and colleagues at UC Berkeley extended that list to 27 different emotions:

- Admiration
- Adoration
- Aesthetic appreciation
- Amusement
- Anxiety
- Awe
- Awkwardness
- Boredom
- Calmness

- Confusion
- Craving
- Disgust
- Empathetic pain
- Entrancement
- Envy
- Excitement
- Fear
- Horror
- Interest

- Joy
- Nostalgia
- Romance
- Sadness
- Satisfaction
- Sexual desire
- Sympathy
- Triumph

This week, identify your feelings. Stop what you're doing at least five times a day (ideally in mid-action, using an automatic reminder, like a calendar notification or alarm) and take a moment to observe how you feel and where you feel it, as you did in the prompt on page 4. Pick out up to three emotions that describe how you feel. You can use the list above, or choose from your own developing emotional vocabulary.

WEEK 3

TYPE: Spiritual

Affirmations are like planting seeds in the ground. First they germinate, then they sprout roots, and then they shoot up through the ground. It takes some time to go from a seed to a full-grown plant. And so it is with affirmations—it takes some time from the first declaration to the final demonstration. Be patient.

—LOUISE L. HAY

Goal: Recognize the power of the words you use, the thoughts you think, and the ability you have to create the life you want through the ways you express yourself.

Is there something in your life that isn't working for you right now? How do you talk to yourself about this aspect of your life? Write down the words you use and the phrases you say.

This week, you will write your own affirmations. Affirmations can state what is already working in your life or assert how you would like your life to be. Follow these guidelines to write your affirmation :

1. Use the present tense ("Today I will . . .").

2. Avoid contractions (keep your words powerful).

3. Use "I" statements and action words ("I can . . ." "I have . . ." "I am . . .").

4. Identify the situation you want to have ("My partner is . . . My heart is . . . My family is. . ."), and build it accordingly (in the present tense).

If you're looking for ideas, start by recognizing things in your life that you've been overlooking. Or consider aspirations and goals you have for different areas of your life or hopes you have for the coming months. Structure these desires as affirmations and help the garden grow.

Using a separate sheet of paper or this week's entry, write three affirmations each day this week.

WEEK 4

Each person deserves a day away in which no problems are confronted, no solutions searched for.

—MAYA ANGELOU

Goal: Intentionally plan a rest. Create a space that is a break from distractions like work, media, family or friend obligations, and electronics. By creating this pause, you can better restore your mind and body.

Recall a time when you had quality rest. Maybe a midday nap, a staycation, or just daydreaming or meditating undisturbed for 10 minutes. Recall this time and remember how it impacted you.

Continued >

Schedule an intentional rest. For example, my family and I take a screen break from sundown Friday to sundown Saturday. We don't go on screens, make phone calls, or check emails. It's a wonderful part of the week. I have a client who puts a 30-minute lunch on her calendar every day, and her work colleagues know that's sacred time. Another colleague meditates twice a day at the office for 15 minutes, creating their own space for downtime.

How can you schedule rest this week? Take a media break for one day this weekend or perhaps a portion of the day? Schedule quiet time into your day for 10 minutes three times this week? Take a mental health day where your only plan is not to have a plan and to just be? However you'd like to do it, intentionally plan your rest, commit to it, and gift yourself that time.

WEEK 5

Being deeply loved by someone gives you strength, while loving someone deeply gives you courage.

—LAO TZU

Goal: This week you will acknowledge the love you feel. By articulating your love recognizing and acknowledging it—you will increase the love you feel and the love that is felt by another.

Can you recall a time someone said "I love you" to you? A mother, a child, a friend? Can you recall how this felt in your body? Put yourself back in the moment and recall the details of the experience.

Think of the people in your life and identify three you'd like to express your love to. This is not the ordinary "Love you, bye" when you're ending a phone call. It is a deeper declaration of how you feel.

When you consider the people you'd like to share this experience with, think about the different types of love, whether romantic love, sibling love, or deep friendship.

Consider the person you love and think about your relationship. Think about how you actively love them and how they love you. Perhaps you'll recall a time they were there for you, or maybe it's something that has nothing to do with you—but something you noticed about the way they are in the world. Reach out to the person in real time, either in person, through a written letter, via a video chat, or over the phone. Take a few moments to articulate your thoughts and feelings. This can be hard, even scary! You are being vulnerable and honest. Note how you feel throughout the process and after you're done.

WEEK 6

TYPE: Mental

If your ship doesn't come in, swim out to meet it.

—JONATHAN WINTERS

Goal: Surprise yourself with abilities that you didn't even know you had. By revealing your courage and acting on it with intention, you might find that you are more capable than you realize. Repeat this practice with regularity and create a habit of courage.

Recall a time when you were afraid, a time when you felt a deeply rooted fear and took action despite the fear. What happened afterward? How did that impact you?

Continued >

Whether you choose to ski, create a piece of art, speak in public, or reach out to an old connection, this is the week to do something difficult, perhaps even something you've been avoiding. Have you always wanted to take a singing or a chess lesson but felt too nervous? Is there someone you'd love to ask on a date but haven't had the courage to approach? Have you let down a friend and need to make it right but have been avoiding the uncomfortable conversation?

This week, take on three of those challenges, ideally something physical, something social, and something emotional. By rising to each of these challenges, you'll grow your courage in different and complementary ways. And remember, the goal here is the action, not the result. So if your art isn't "great" or your friend doesn't accept your apology, that's okay. This week is about taking action, not the response to that action.

TYPE: Mental

I am resourceful. I can provide what I need for myself. I can work, I can earn, I can live within my means. I can create a healthy financial ecosystem. I am doing my best. My level of earning is what is right for me.

Goal: Make an honest assessment of your financial situation. If you're financially healthy, acknowledge (and celebrate) that. If you don't know where you are moneywise, have been avoiding facing your financial situation, or know that you're in bad fiscal shape, take this week to peel back the covers and see what's going on.

What does "being financially resilient" mean to you? How much is enough? On a scale of 1 (not enough) to 10 (more than enough), how content are you with your ability to make, spend, and save money? Rank each of these three categories separately.

Examine your fiscal health. Take a look at what is in your wallet or bank account. Consider any debt you've accrued or paid off (or simply observe your lack of debt, if that's your situation!). Have a look at what you've spent, what you've earned, and what you've saved, if anything, over the last three months. Write these numbers down.

How would you assess your financial health?

Now, take a look at what you've earned over the last three years (if you haven't been in an earning position, consider how the money has been flowing into and out of your household). How have you spent it, and what have you saved? Write this down as well. You can write down the broad strokes on the back of a napkin or get more granular on a spreadsheet—whatever helps you take action.

Do you want to shift the way you spend, save, or earn? What is working, and what will you modify? How will you modify it, and when can you start? Figure out your destination and how your money can help you reach those goals. Record it in some form, save it, and put a prompt in your calendar to take a look at this in six months (or at a time that is more relevant to your established goal).

WEEK 8

Agriculture changes the landscape more than anything else we do. It alters the composition of species. We don't realize it when we sit down to eat, but that is our most profound engagement with the rest of nature.

—MICHAEL POLLAN

Goal: To generate an awareness of the circle of life, and your part in the production and consumption of life, gain a deeper understanding of food systems and how what you consume becomes part of you.

What are some of your favorite ingredients? What meals do you love to eat? What do you love to cook? What meals do you like to share with others?

Continued >

Before you eat, take a moment to consider one item on your plate and what went into it appearing there. Perhaps it's a lemon that you picked off the tree in your backyard. Who planted the tree, what pollinators created the lemon, what bugs may have tried to eat the fruit before you? Who stopped them? Who packaged your food so that it could end up on a shelf where you bought it? Who stocked the shelf?

Take a mindful trip like that with one item on your plate before each meal. Allow yourself to feel connected to the food chain that created, grew, harvested, transported, and prepared the food so that it could be on your plate . . . and ultimately, a part of your body!

TYPE: Spiritual

I am part of the world. I am in concert with other creatures, from tiny bacteria to the enormous blue whale. I have creatures living inside me and all around me. I am part of a larger whole. I am aware of my connectedness with other living things.

Goal: Connect yourself to the larger whole of other living creatures. See the world around you as alive and filled with other living creatures. Consider your role in this world as connected, supported, and contributing.

Take a look around you. What is the first living thing you see? What is something alive, within arm's reach, that perhaps you cannot see? What living things are visible out the window or living in the ground beneath you? What is the largest living thing that you could walk to and touch within the next 10 minutes?

Go into nature and take a journal (maybe even this one!) to record what you see. Find the smallest living creature around you (insects count!), and then identify the largest one. Find at least 10 animals (humans are animals) and 10 trees, flowers, or shrubs. Extra points if you are able to find a flying animal, a swimming animal, and a walking, crawling, or slithering land animal. Identify them by name if you can. Draw a picture or write down three interesting things about the living creatures you see. Consider your role in this community of living things.

TYPE: Social

A little consideration, a little thought for others, makes all the difference.

—A. A. MILNE

Goal: Identify and recognize the people who support you in your life. Allow yourself to feel held and loved by these people who are rooting for you every day.

Who are the five people you spend the most time with? These can be family members, friends, coworkers, or even commuting buddies. How much waking time per week do you spend with these people?

Continued >

Take a few moments each day this week to identify the people who are part of your life, though not in your immediate friend or family group. First, start with your medical or caregiving team (like your pharmacist, primary care doctor, eye doctor, chiropractor, acupuncturist, therapist, etc.). Then consider your physical team (massage therapist, yoga classmates, walking buddy, etc.). Next, think about the people who help you eat (grocery clerk, butcher, farmer, food delivery person, barista, etc.).

Picture the faces of the people you know, and, ideally, name them if you can. If you don't know their names, ask them the next time you see them. Next, consider your community (your neighbors, folks you see walking the dog, your auto mechanic, your plumber, your accountant, etc).

For the last three days of the week, list your friends, family members, and colleagues.

These are the people in your life. If you like, using a separate sheet of paper, draw a sketch of your social networks (we're talking actual human beings here with names and faces, not anonymous social media "followers") to give beautiful expression to all the people who support you and whom you support in turn.

TYPE: Social

To send a letter is a good way to go somewhere without moving anything but your heart.

—PHYLLIS THEROUX

Goal: Intentionally rebuild a powerful connection that has become dormant. By reigniting this once powerful connection, and remembering what was, you can bring this connection into the present.

Think back to when you were a child in elementary, middle, or high school. Think back to the people who shaped you: teachers, coaches, caregivers, faith or religious leaders, friends' parents, parents' friends. Make a list of five people from your childhood who impacted your life.

Choose one person from the list who impacted you in a positive way. This week, take some time to write a letter to that person, letting them know the impact they had on you. Take your time to recall some specific memories and experiences, and share how those experiences led to choices that had a direct impact on your life and character—who you are today. If possible, meet with them in person to read the letter, read it to them aloud on the phone or via video chat, or send the letter via the post in your very own handwriting.

The act of writing your memory and your gratitude can reveal powerful emotions. Communicating in real time can be powerful as well. This exercise is a client favorite. Prepare to move, be moved, and connect deeply. Be sure to give your chosen person the letter after you've recited it because they will want to reread it, as the emotions of the moment can be overwhelming.

TYPE: Mental

I care for myself through regular, healthful sleep. This is a time for my body and mind to rest, repair, and restore. My sleep quality impacts my mental and physical health. I have the sleep I need.

Goal: Evaluate your sleep hygiene, both going to bed and awakening from sleep. Evaluate your current setup and confirm that your sleep system is sound, or find ways to improve it.

How would you say your sleep was last night on a scale of 1 (not good) to 10 (great)? When was the last time you got a great night's sleep?

Continued >

Take a look at your sleep practices and evaluate them on a 3-point scale (1=yes; 2=maybe; 3=no).

_ I have at least one screen-free hour before bedtime.
_ My body is in bed for at least 7 to 9 hours.
_ My bedroom is dark and cool.
_ I have adequate pillows and covers, and they are clean.
_ I get into my bed with a clean body, teeth, clothes, and hair.
_ I am able to sleep through the night.
_ My digital devices are not in my room.
_ My bedroom has adequate ventilation.
_ My bedroom is quiet (or I sleep with a noise machine).
_ My sleep routine is peaceful; I fall asleep with ease.
_ My alarm (if I use one) wakes me gently with tones or illumination.
_ I can recall dreams on occasion.

Your score:

12–19: Healthy sleep is yours!

20–27: Your sleep could be improved. Shift your 3s to 1s by keeping phones out of the bedroom or trying a gratitude exercise before bedtime. Next week's exercise will help with this.

28–36: You can radically improve your health with better sleep. Start with the basics: Make sure that your body is in bed, screen-free, for a full 8 hours.

TYPE: Emotional

I choose where I put my attention. I take responsibility for the thoughts I choose to spend time on. My mind is active and curious, and I can guide it to the areas where I want to focus.

Goal: You have wonderful experiences every day. Waking up is a wonderful experience. Eating food, seeing sunshine, and even taking a shower can be a blissed-out experience if you choose for it to be. This week, focus on the wonderful moments you experience each day.

Take a look at your day so far. Maybe your day started 15 minutes ago, or maybe you've been awake for many hours. Look back and think about one great thing that happened today. Recall it, relive it.

This week's exercise is called "Three Good Things" and was popularized by UC Berkeley's Greater Good Science Center.

Each day, at the end of the day, recall something good that happened that day. It could have been a juicy peach you ate, with its juices dripping down your face, or a bright red cardinal that you saw out your window after a snowstorm.

When you recall the event, take your time with it. Set a timer for 2½ minutes, and return yourself to the exact moment; let yourself live it again. Remember what you were doing at the time, who you were with. Give it context and detail. And, most importantly, let yourself feel the feelings again—the delight, the joy, the satisfaction, the good.

If you like, you can also take a few minutes to record the experience verbally or write it down in this week's entry or on a separate sheet of paper. By recalling the experience in detail, you are better able to feel the emotions of the moment again. Repeat this exercise five times this week.

WEEK 14

I'm not afraid of storms, for I'm learning how to sail my ship.

—LOUISA MAY ALCOTT

Goal: When you are a child, you are a professional learner. As an adult, your learning tends to slow down. This week, reconnect with the joy of learning.

What is something you loved doing as a kid? Something that perhaps you're not doing anymore or not nearly as often? Dressing up in costumes? Doing magic tricks? Singing into a hairbrush and dancing around your room? Remind yourself of this thing you used to do and got lost in.

Continued >

Learning invigorates your brain and gives you the opportunity to practice and develop a skill. As you fall deeper into an interest or hobby, you have a new way to engage with the world and with other people who have similar interests.

Is there something you've been thinking about learning? A new language? Playing the piano? Bird-watching? Terrarium building? Calligraphy? Knitting? When you give yourself the time and space to pursue an interest, you forge new neural connections. You may experience flow state and increasing levels of mastery, which are joyful in and of themselves and help you develop confidence.

Identify a hobby you'd like to learn more about, and dedicate five hours this week to that hobby. Give yourself extra points if you pursue something you've been thinking about for a while.

TYPE: Mental

*We don't see things as they are, we see them
as we are.*

—ANAÏS NIN

Goal: Identify three modes of storytelling: pessimist, optimist, realist. Play with the modes, acknowledging that you can choose and shift your outlook at any given time.

When you tell yourself stories about your life, do you have a tendency to spin your stories in a way that's positive, negative, or just the facts? When you look at your day today, what do you see?

This week we will practice using three different lenses: pessimism (looking at what could go wrong, framing negatively), optimism (seeing what could go right, with a positive spin), and realism (unemotional perspective, fact-based).

First, look at something you'll be doing today—perhaps going to the beach, giving a presentation, or making dinner for friends. The optimist will imagine a sunny day, an easy drive, a clean beach. The pessimist will envision a terrible speech, technical difficulties, a disrespectful audience, and negative feedback after the talk. The realist will think about the friends who will be coming, the food that will be prepared, and the way they'd like to set the table.

Each day this week, consider a situation that you are in, and spend a few moments seeing it through each of these lenses. Record your storytelling from each lens into a microphone, or write it down in this week's entry or on a separate sheet of paper. Which lens do you naturally gravitate to? Play with perspective this week, and observe how shifting the story you tell yourself shifts your experience.

TYPE: Spiritual

I can regulate my emotions. I can feel happy, anxious, confident, sad, or serene. I can feel my feelings and shift them as I choose. I am emotionally agile.

Goal: Use nature to support your emotional regulation. Intentionally engage with the natural world to bring yourself into the present and enjoy an aesthetically engaging experience.

"Forest bathing" is the idea that by surrounding yourself in nature, you can reduce and alleviate stress. What kind of natural surroundings do you retreat to when you want to increase your calm?

Continued >

These three tools will help you regulate your emotions in nature. Try one or try them all.

1. **Nature breathing.** Observe a blade of grass, a branch on a tree, or a petal on a flower. The goal is to focus on something alive that is not in motion and of which there are several. Engage in a breathing meditation; look at one leaf and breathe in, another and breathe out. Continue this nature breathing meditation for as long as you like.

2. **Olfactory investigation.** Nature gives off all kinds of smells. Burning leaves carry a distinct scent, as do wet grass and a rain shower on a hot day. Purposefully seek out scents in nature; see if you can find a dozen different ones.

3. **Five senses, six dimensions.** As ambulatory beings, we tend to spend more time experiencing what is in front of us than what is beneath, above, to the left, right, and behind us. It makes sense; those are the directions in which we move. We are less observant of what's above us, unless there's something that catches our attention, like a skyscraper or a plane. When in nature, use all five senses in six dimensions. Listen for the soundscape in all directions, visualize what is around you, feel it, taste it (if possible), and smell it (as with the exercise above).

I care for my body and my mind. I check in with my body and listen when it talks to me. If my body needs more than I can provide, I can call upon those who will help me.

Goal: Organize your health check-ins. Prioritize and schedule your regular appointments, and identify whether or not you'd like additional support.

Who is your favorite health professional? Why do you like this person the most? Is there a type of health professional you've been curious about and might like to try?

Schedule your big three: annual doctor's appointment, dental exam, and eye doctor appointment. Remember, you're just scheduling this week. Feel free to schedule these appointments over the next three, six, or even twelve months; just get them on the calendar. If relevant for you, consider adding a mammogram, colonoscopy, prostate exam, or other check-ups as needed for your situation. If you don't have health insurance, take this week to research local clinics that offer low-cost or no cost services to community members who aren't insured.

Once you've covered the basics, consider additional and complementary health needs. Is there a specialist you might like to check in with or need to see, like an allergist? Might you like to pursue an alternative health provider, like a Reiki practitioner, a massage therapist, or a reflexologist? How about practitioners of acupuncture or other traditional Chinese medicine modalities? What about an Ayurvedic doctor, a psychic, an energy healer, or an astrologist? Consider connecting with a practitioner of at least one complementary approach to health and healing that you've been curious about and have not yet tried.

TYPE: Physical

You cannot always control what goes on outside.
But you can always control what goes on inside.

—WAYNE DYER

Goal: This week, you will observe all that you consume. Try not to avoid items that you would have consumed otherwise; this is a week of honest observation. Be specific about quantity and quality of all that you consume.

What have you consumed today or what do you plan to consume? Make note of all meals and snacks, all food and drinks that you take into your body.

Continued >

The food writer Michael Pollan was famous for writing, "Eat food, not too much, mostly plants." Food scientists, nutritionists, and dietitians around the world have celebrated this simple phrase as a useful, sensible healthy eating plan.

This week you will focus on the foods that you are eating (noting that drinks are "food" for the body, insofar that they can be nourishing and caloric). Using this week's entry or a separate sheet of paper, please keep track of the food, drinks, and other items you consume each day. Note the serving size as well.

Then, take note of how you feel after you eat; do you feel bloated or gassy? Energized or sluggish? Look for trends in what you eat and how you feel. What is or is not serving your body? How might you want to make adjustments moving forward?

TYPE: Physical

I opened two gifts this morning. They were my eyes.

−ZIG ZIGLAR

Goal: Love your body. Appreciate whatever it is about your body that brings you joy, pleasure, and/or contentment.

What is a part of your body that you like? What is a part of your body that you are grateful for? What is a part of your body that gives you joy? Pleasure? Contentment? List these body parts and explore why.

After taking stock of the body parts that bring an assortment of positive feelings, let's give back. Take a look at the body parts that you acknowledged in this week's entry. Feel them if possible. Do they need anything? For example, if you chose your lungs or your heart, are they getting enough action? Are you using them enough, or could they benefit from more exercise? If your hands give you joy, how is the health of your skin? Is it nourished? Are your feet calloused because you use them a lot? Could they use a soak?

Identify how you might want to give the body parts you love the gift of care.

WEEK 20

I breathe every minute of every day. I can speed up my breath or slow it down. I can use my breath to adjust my emotional state. Slow, long breaths help me calm down. I can adjust my breathing pace whenever I choose to.

Goal: Observe your current breathing. Is it shallow? Deep? Try new breathing tools to support self-regulation. Practice this new breathing approach daily.

Many people use their breath to regulate their emotions and support meditation. Do you use any breathing techniques? What are they and how frequently do you use them?

Continued >

Experiment with a technique called "box breathing." To do it, you take a breath in for a count of four, hold it for a count of four, release it for a count of four and hold the exhale for a count of four. Repeat, slowing the count as you go.

If you can, visualize a little box being drawn as you go, line by line. In for four, hold for four, out for four, hold for four, repeat.

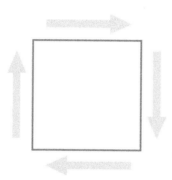

This is a simple breathing method to start. There are others! If you like, extend this breathing exercise by holding a longer release (maybe a count of six, then eight). Lengthening the exhale activates the parasympathetic nervous system and can increase your relaxation.

It is a luxury to be understood.

—RALPH WALDO EMERSON

Goal: Practice active listening. Experience the power of deeply listening to another person, and enjoy the opportunity to be heard.

Can you recall the last time you felt heard? Where were you, and who were you with? What do you think the other person heard, and how do you know they heard you?

Find a partner for this exercise. It can be a close friend or someone you've never met before.

The speaker will speak for two minutes on a topic that is important to them. The listener will set a timer and listen, without speaking at all. Maintain eye contact.

After two minutes, the listener will set a timer for one minute. The listener will share what they heard with the speaker. The speaker will not speak during this period, and eye contact should be maintained.

After that is complete, the listener will set a timer for one minute. The speaker will confirm what the listener heard and correct any misconceptions. They may add to or clarify their earlier comments.

After the exercise is complete, switch roles. After both partners have been listeners and speakers, discuss what the experience was like.

WEEK 22

My life is my choice. I have the power to take my life in the direction I want to go. When I set my intention, I chart my adventure.

Goal: Looking forward to an event can be as enjoyable as experiencing it. Schedule some activities to savor.

Is there anything on your calendar in the coming days or weeks that you're looking forward to? A birthday or get-together? A new season or holiday? Identify it and go a level deeper: Why is this event important to you?

Continued >

Plan something you'd like to do this week, this month, and for the following three seasons. For ideas, consider holidays, your birthday, friends' special occasions, anniversaries, or seasonal changes (plant flowers, go to the beach, hike in nature, plan a leaf-peeping trip).

Intentionally plan something to look forward to, whether it's a trip, a meaningful purchase, a night with friends, or a date with yourself. This week's goal is to savor, so remember that this is about looking forward to something and not the destination. Enjoy savoring what's to come.

TYPE: Social

Those who are happiest are those who do the most for others.

—BOOKER T. WASHINGTON

Goal: Share your gift with someone who needs it. Maybe it's a smile or a hug, your ability to read, your time, your love and kindness, or some disposable income to help another person out. Helping others is good for you because it increases your sense of contributing to the greater good.

Look for another living being who could use some help. A dog that needs a walk, a child who needs a playmate, a person that needs a meal. Identify three beings who need something today. What might you offer them from your gifts?

Seek opportunities to help someone. These opportunities are all around you, all the time. Someone who is having a hard time might just need a smile; someone carrying packages will appreciate that you open the door. An elderly or overloaded neighbor might be thrilled to have you shovel their driveway or mow their lawn; the person sitting outside your coffee shop who doesn't have a home might appreciate that you offer to buy them breakfast and stop to have a conversation.

WEEK 24

TYPE: Mental

I am alive, and to be alive means to be in a constant state of change. Even as I sit still, my heart beats, my lungs take in air, my blood flows. I embrace change.

Goal: Recognize that the only constant is change. Intentionally chart a course for the years ahead of you. And recognize that your course will shift as opportunities arise.

How old are you? How many years has it been since you became an adult, whether in mind or in body? If you lived to be 100, what percentage of your adult life have you lived until now? How is it going so far?

Continued >

Chart your course, decade by decade. Find a couple of blank pieces of paper and a pen. Write the decade that you are currently in at the top of the page. On the next page, write the next decade, and so on and so on, until you hit your nineties.

Under each decade, list some milestones you'd like to reach in that decade, like "travel to Africa," "foster a dog," "write a book," and so on. If relevant, you may want to list the ages of your parents, children, close family, or dear friends in addition to your decade. For instance you might write, "My parents celebrate 50 years together" or even "Celebrate a 10-year friendiversary" for those relationships that aren't bio-logical but are highly valued. This will help you keep in mind your milestones as well as those of the people you love.

TYPE: Social

There are always flowers for those who want to see them.

—HENRI MATISSE

Goal: Increase your awareness of life by inviting life into your home. Feel more alive and connected to living energy and enjoy the presence of vitality.

Go outside first thing in the morning. Take 10 minutes to look for and listen to living beings. Do you hear birds, see trees? Cars (driven by people)? A train passing by sounding its whistle? The gentle clap of lapping waves? Intentionally look for and listen to life. If possible, repeat this outing each morning this week.

Invite life into your home and into your daily existence. Consider inviting a furry friend over for a visit, or perhaps adopt a fish or a new plant. Or take a look at the life that already exists around you. What kind of animals live near you, right in your (shared) backyard? Pigeons? Deer? Foxes? If you're in an apartment complex, do you hear, see, and sense other people?

Consider adding new life to your home; it can be as unobtrusive as a succulent or a terrarium. Reflect with new eyes on the vitality that is already present in your life.

WEEK 26

My body is my temple. The items I consume influence my health and energy. I will deny entrance for items that harm me. I can source nourishment that helps me thrive.

Goal: Generate awareness of the items you consume that can have a negative impact on your body.

What items do you put into your body that can have a physiological impact on your system? These can be items you are allergic or semi-allergic to, as well as caffeine, prescribed and unprescribed drugs, sugar, alcohol, or processed foods.

Continued >

This week, either in this week's entry or on a separate sheet of paper, write down the items you consume that can have a negative physical or mental impact on your body. Now, of course, if you drink too much water or eat too many apples, that can make you sick. I'm not talking about food items like that; I'm talking about items that are known toxins.

Tracking your consumption (like you did in Week 18) can help you pay attention to what you put into your body. A daily cup of coffee can easily become two, or three. And a supersized coffee late in the day, to help you cope with the sleepless night before, can unfortunately lead to a sleepless night thereafter.

At the end of the week, what trends do you see? How is your sugar, processed food, and other mind- or mood-altering food consumption? Are you comfortable with where it is, or might you want to make some changes?

TYPE: Emotional

Every now and then it's good to stop climbing and appreciate the view from right where you are.

—LORI DESCHENE

Goal: Reflect on your accomplishments and experiences from the past year. Reconnect with the emotions associated with these experiences.

Consider your last month. What stands out in your memory that you enjoyed? Celebrated? Achieved? Felt in your body? Did you share this with someone? Write down two or three vivid memories from the past month of your life.

Take a few pieces of paper and label them with the months of the year. If you have one handy, you may want to use a blank calendar from the past year.

First, go through and mark down any big events from the past year—weddings, anniversaries, birthdays, and so forth. Mark events you attended in real time with others (in person or via Zoom or other connecting software), reunions, or holidays. Take a moment to recount these events.

Then reflect on your achievements—did you run a 5K? Reach another goal? Start a new job? End a relationship that wasn't serving you? You'll find that memories of the year start to flow back. (Feel free to look at your planner to jog your memory.)

When you're done, take a moment to sit with each month and reflect on the emotions you associate with your experiences. (If you find yourself searching to describe it, feel free to use the list of emotions provided in Week 2, page 6.) Remember how those emotions (felt in the body) became feelings (a conscious awareness in the brain). Fill your heart and mind with your feelings and emotions from the past year of your life.

WEEK 28

Time is our most valuable nonrenewable resource, and if we want to treat it with respect, we need to set priorities.

—ALBERT-LÁSZLÓ BARABÁSI

Goal: Break free of passive social media habits. Return hours to your day by ending passive engagement with social media and removing pings and reminders from your life. If you don't use social media, consider another mindless habit that you want to discontinue.

Remove social media apps from your phone for this week. Facebook, TikTok, Twitter, Instagram, Snapchat . . . and whatever has been invented since this journal was published. Turn off all notifications on your phone. Now, take note of how you fill that time once it's reclaimed. What do you gravitate to when these distractions are subtracted? How do you feel?

Continued >

Observe the intrusiveness of social media, and take an intentional break from passive social media engagement.

Once you've removed social media from your phone, you can use it, intentionally, once a day for up to 30 minutes on a desktop or tablet. Consider using email for up to 30 minutes three times a day (or select another finite, specific amount of time with a clear boundary that works for you and your needs). Social media is designed to move into our lives and stay there, interrupting us from other activities and keeping us engaged with it and detached from ourselves.

Increase your awareness of your social media habits. Make a conscious choice to experience the world beyond the screens. If you're addressing another habit—common culprits include nail biting, snacking, TV watching, or complaining— observe the mindless intrusion and take stock.

TYPE: Social

In my humble opinion, non-cooperation with evil is as much a duty as is cooperation with good.

—MAHATMA GANDHI

Goal: Assess your -isms. Increase your awareness of your biases.

When is the last time you can remember being treated differently because of your age, size, gender, identity, race, ability, sexual preference, or other inherent quality? Recall the situation in detail, especially how it made you feel. If you are feeling as if this doesn't apply to you, have you heard about it happening to someone else? Recall that experience, as if you were that person, to help you consider another's perspective.

Become aware of your unconscious biases. Take stock of your biases so that you can bring them into view and address them. This can include racism, heterosexism, gender bias, ableism, ageism, or discrimination against minorities or immigrants. There are many more biases, so feel free to keep going.

Each day, pick a bias and ask yourself the following questions:

1. What biases might I have toward people in this demographic?

2. What impact does this have on my relationship with _____? (Ideally, choose a person you know who's in this demographic, or someone who is impacted by your bias.)

3. How can I shift my thinking to avoid bias? How can I shift my behavior?

WEEK 30

I am strong, and I am kind. I have dreams, and I can make them come true. I can do hard things. My life is filled with challenges that make me stronger. I am my friend.

Goal: Develop self-compassion. Access gentleness and kindness, and direct it toward yourself.

When you consider the voice you use to speak to yourself, how would you describe it? Harsh and demanding? Soft and indulgent? Generous and kind? Consider this voice.

Continued >

Find or draw a picture of yourself when you were young. If you have something from your childhood, like a piece of art that you made, a favorite doll, or a piece of clothing, you can use that too. Consider that child with fresh eyes, as if you were just meeting. Take a look at this child or a picture that they have drawn. What do you see? The innocence? The fresh perspective? Imagine a conversation with them. What would you discuss?

Embrace this child with your heart.

Practice talking to yourself with the loving, compassionate voice that you would use with a child. You are the child; the child is you. Consciously use the gentle, kind voice of compassion when you speak to yourself. Love yourself as you would this child. The child is still in you.

TYPE: Mental

It is the simple things of life that make living worth-while, the sweet fundamental things such as love and duty, work and rest, and living closer to nature.

—LAURA INGALLS WILDER

Goal: Recognize the small efforts you make every day. Acknowledge the effort that can sometimes go unseen. Amplify the small wins.

For this week, identify something big that you achieved over the last few years (things like a job promotion, taking up a new creative skill, buying a house, etc.). Identify five small, yet vital, actions that impacted your ability to make the larger accomplishment a reality.

In this week's entry or on a separate sheet of paper, track your small accomplishments each day. They may appear mundane, and that's the point. Look for the little things you do each day that contribute to your mental, physical, social, or emotional health. Take three minutes each day to write them down. Set a timer and write out the list. Feel free to continue listing after the timer sounds; just be sure to spend at least three minutes on this exercise.

Rome wasn't built in a day, and neither is your life. Take a look at the pebbles you put in place as you move toward your personal milestones. Did you wake up? Get out of bed? Walk your dog? Call a friend? Drink eight glasses of water during the day?

Recognize your small wins and accomplishments this week. Small positive actions accumulate quickly. Acknowledge yours.

TYPE: Emotional

My dreams are limitless, and I can create anything I choose to. I am full of ideas that I can bring to fruition. My brain is fertile, and I am capable.

Goal: Use visualization techniques to identify a specific goal in the future.

Look at your life as it is today. Which parts of it are in line with your hopes for yourself? Which parts exceed the hopes you had for yourself?

Continued >

Set a goal. Any goal. Three sets of 15 push-ups each day for a week? Win an Academy Award? Greet each person you see with a smile? Adopt a chihuahua? Identify a goal, with a specific and measurable time frame so that you know when you've achieved it. Make sure the goal feels meaningful to you. Take a look at your "future life" ideas from Week 24 (page 72) to see if you want to hone in on something you wrote about there, or perhaps you have a new idea.

Once you have a goal in mind, write it down on a separate piece of paper, along with the time frame for achieving it.

Envision what your life will look like after achieving your goal. Picture yourself with the goal achieved. What is different? How are you different? What is the impact of having reached your goal, both for yourself and for others? Draw a picture about this moment, or write a story about it.

Revise or refine your goal accordingly, then commit to it. You'll know you've hit the right one when you can feel the tangible impact of achieving your goal.

TYPE: Spiritual

I have learned that as long as I hold fast to my beliefs and values—and follow my own moral compass—then the only expectations I need to live up to are my own.

—MICHELLE OBAMA

Goal: Examine your character more deeply. Consider who you are, and what your values are, so that you can feel more free to be yourself.

When you think about a person's character, what comes to mind? When you think about your character, how would you describe yourself? What do you value?

According to the VIA Institute on Character, "Character strengths are the positive parts of your personality that make you feel authentic and engaged." The list that follows includes the 24 strengths that are the focus of the VIA Institute.

Take a look at the list and circle the character strengths that resonate with you. Feel free to add your own if you like. Now edit this list down to five. Then organize the five attributes in order of importance. How do you live out these character strengths on a daily basis? How might you live them more fully?

Honesty	Love
Appreciation of Beauty	Creativity
& Excellence	Hope
Fairness	Prudence
Humor	Leadership
Kindness	Perseverance
Judgment	Love of Learning
Zest	Spirituality
Curiosity	Forgiveness
Gratitude	Teamwork
Perspective	Self-Regulation
Social Intelligence	Humility
Bravery	

WEEK 34

I am unique. I am the only person who has experienced the life I have had. I have something unique to offer the world that only I can contribute.

Goal: Embrace your creativity. Find a medium that you would like to explore and give it a try. Dig in and see if you can get into a creative flow state.

Each person creates every day, from an outfit they assemble, to their hairstyle, to their meals and more. How are you creative? How do you define creativity?

Continued >

First, think about what you might like to create this week: Would you like to paint a room, wrap a present, write a poem, try out an adult coloring book? Use food coloring to color some snow, or make a shower sculpture with shaving cream? Take a trip to an art store for inspiration, or just look around your house and see what you can create with items you have on hand. You might make a birdfeeder from an old milk container and some toilet paper tubes or a jewelry organizer from an egg carton. Feel free to look online for some creative inspiration. Get creative in whatever medium you choose.

WEEK 35

I take responsibility for my environment. I care for my body, my home, and my planet. I know the environment in which I function best, and I will make every effort to create it.

Goal: Improve your living environments: your home space, work space, and travel space (car, bicycle, feet). Improve the environment so that you can be more relaxed and effective.

When was the last time you came home and felt great about your space? Describe how your home looked and felt to you. It's okay if it's been a while.

Over the last few years, we've heard a lot about "the life-changing magic of tidying up," as one popular same-titled book put it. This is your week to see what all the hype is about. Many people use spring as a reason to open up the windows and clean out the place, but those who celebrate Christmas use the next day, called "Boxing Day," to rehome items no longer needed. Cultures around the world have their own terms and time for it, but no matter the specifics, cleaning is universal.

Find one area that you'd like to clean up. It could be your sock drawer, your closet, or the glove compartment of your car. Take everything out of that area. Then give it a good cleaning.

Separate the items you've removed into three piles: garbage, give away/sell, and keep. Try to keep only that which is meaningful or useful, preferably both.

Complete this exercise in three different locations this week. Try to improve one area in your home, another in your work or study space, and another in your travel space. If you feel stuck on this one, start with a small and simple space—your pockets!

WEEK 36

Look past your thoughts so you may drink the pure nectar of this moment.

—RUMI

Goal: Intentionally create an awe-inspiring experience. Deliberately build an experience to feel a sense of wonder. Gain the tools to build awe in your life more regularly.

What does the word "awe" mean to you? How about "awesome", or "awe-inspiring"? When was the last time you were awed?

Continued >

Many people are awed by natural beauty (mountains, trees, lakes), but others are moved by other intangible presences. I was deeply awed staring at a peony after a six-hour silent meditation. Was it the peony or the way I prepared myself to see it?

This week, create an experience like that for yourself. If possible, put yourself in a natural environment that is already a part of your life (your yard, your stoop, or a bench in a local park). Your objective is to find something simple, take some time with it, and observe it in a deeper way. Give yourself 45 minutes to walk around and slowly, deeply observe your environment. You can spend the entire time staring at blades of grass or observing the small insects that live in the grass. Or look to the trees to find a nest and perhaps a baby bird. Might you be able to see a feeding? Or people-watch. Notice how people carry themselves and their things, or how they interact with each other and the world around them.

Look at the environment that surrounds you with fresh eyes for the awe-inspiring beauty you've maybe not noticed before.

WEEK 37

My body can enjoy motion. I can stretch, bob my head, or tap my feet. Movement impacts my body in a positive way. I know how to move my body in a way that brings me pleasure.

Goal: Identify enjoyable movement moments. Increase physical activity by increasing the availability of enjoyable activities.

Think about something you liked to do with your body when you were a child. Did you like to swing? Climb? Smile a big smile? Maybe you liked to put on goggles in the bathtub and play under water? Make snow angels? How did you enjoy moving your body?

Exercise is an important tool for health and self-care. By stretching, strengthening, and raising our heart rate regularly, we can improve our overall wellness.

Find a way to move your body. Is it dancing? Walking? Stretching or having someone else stretch your body for you? Consider how you enjoy moving your body, and commit to trying something new this week. Or return an old favorite to your repertoire.

WEEK 38

I decide what feels best for me. I am respectful of my needs and my boundaries. I am respectful of others' needs and boundaries too. Communicating those boundaries is something I can do.

Goal: Consider boundaries that help you feel comfortable being touched or touching others. Within the context of your relationships with others, what words can you say that will help clarify what kind of touch is okay and what kind is not?

Think about the last time you felt positive touch. Maybe it was a puppy curling up in your lap, cuddling with a loved one, or holding hands with a friend.

Continued >

It is socially appropriate (and appreciated) to ask someone permission before you touch them. You ask before you hug a person, and, due to events like the coronavirus pandemic, many of us have reduced the frequency of our handshaking. Before you touch someone else, be sure to ask for and receive permission.

This week, practice asking. For the sake of habit building, ask any living thing if you can touch them. Before you pet a dog, ask, "May I touch you?" and observe their body language to see if they are comfortable. Before you pick up a baby, ask permission from them—as well as their caregiver. Proceed with care and notice how they are responding to your touch.

By asking, you are letting yourself and the other person know that you respect their physical space, boundaries, and sovereignty—ownership of their body. It is a deep act of respect for the other person and for yourself.

Real listening is a willingness to let the other person change you.

—ALAN ALDA

Goal: Take a look at your relationships and identify those relationships that replenish you and those that may be depleting you.

Think through your relationships, whether it's with members of your family, your friends, a romantic partner, professional colleagues, or others. Who "fills your cup"? Why did you choose this person? List three to five people who fill your cup in different, or perhaps complementary, ways.

Relationships change over time. Although there's a powerful cultural myth that friendships are forever, that isn't always so. Some friendships are wonderful for a time, need a break, and can begin again in a new way, but others may come for a season and that may be enough. As with fashion, some styles are classic and enduring while others are more of a brief trend. The same can be said for relationships.

Take a look at your relationship inventory from Week 10 (page 28) with fresh eyes. Now consider each of these relationships. Mentally rank your satisfaction with them on a scale of 1 ("empties my cup") to 5 ("fills my cup").

Once you've evaluated these relationships, consider how you may want to reduce some of the time spent in relationships that are sapping your energy and how you may also want to increase your availability to those that are energizing.

WEEK 40

I am alive. My heart beats; my cells multiply. My body is alive and vital. My spirit or soul is also alive, though more difficult to measure tangibly. I am alive in different ways, living in multiple dimensions.

Goal: Intentionally seek out a fresh start, a creative beginning. Recognize the freshness and possibility of a new moment.

What is your origin story? Feel free to tell any meaningful story you choose. This can be your birth; your rebirth; the genesis of your identity; becoming an adult, a professional, a partner, or a parent. Share an origin story that resounds deeply with you.

Continued >

While some believe that life has a clear beginning and end, others believe life is never-ending, that energy and life can neither be created nor destroyed. This week, seek out a beginning—whether it's a sunrise, the first person you greet during the day, the first star in the sky, or lighting a fresh wick on a candle. See if you can witness the birth of a living being: a puppy or a horse, a baby chick pecking through her eggshell, or a butterfly emerging from a chrysalis. There are lots of videos you can find online. Intentionally observe the emergence of life and the energy shift that it brings.

TYPE: Physical

Good sleep is vital for my body. I can prepare for good sleep with a healthy bedtime routine that I enjoy and look forward to. I can parent myself, tuck myself in, and show great care and kindness to my body, spirit, and mind with a healthy pre-sleep routine.

Goal: Observe your evening routine and how you intentionally welcome rest. Determine what is working and what can be improved.

What helps you fall asleep? What helps settle your mind and soothe you, preparing you for a good night of sleep? List five tools you could use and how they might help you.

Answer the following self-reflection questions to see how your evening routine is or isn't helping you settle into a restful period of sleep.

- Observe and record your actions in the last hour before bed at least two to three times this week.

- Is your sleep routine consistent during the week and weekend? If so, how? If not, why not? What is the range of sleep times you have?

- What are your hygiene habits before bed? This can include washing your body, hands, and face; brushing and flossing your teeth; brushing your hair, etc. How long do you give yourself for this routine?

- Do you read or meditate before going to bed?

- Do you take any medication or supplements before heading to bed?

- What do you eat and drink during the last two hours before bedtime?

- What physical activity do you have in the two hours before bedtime? Exercise? Stretching? Yoga?

- What are your screen habits before bedtime? When do you "shut down," and where are your screens while you sleep?

TYPE: Physical

I can choose how I welcome each day. I can impact the day ahead by connecting with my body and mind, listening to what I need. I can greet each new day, each new opportunity, as I choose.

Goal: Recognize what's working well with your morning routine and how you might improve it. Create a morning routine that sets you up for the day you'd like to have.

What do you notice first thing when you wake up? Your body? The light in the room? Birdsong? What typically wakes you up in the morning? What's the difference between a good wake-up and a not-so-good wake-up?

Continued >

For the first two days of the week, observe your sensory wake-up. How does your body feel? What is the temperature and air quality of the room? Listen to the noises that are welcoming you out of slumber. Are they pleasant or jarring? Whom do you connect with and how? What is the taste in your mouth? At what point do you reach for a screen? Coffee? Tea? Water? Bathroom? Shower?

For the next three days, intentionally observe the first 15 minutes of your awakening, especially focusing on your self-talk. Are you smiling or grimacing? What are you saying to yourself, and how is that impacted by your experiences getting up? What experiences are mandatory, and what experiences are you choosing as part of your morning routine?

For the rest of the week, consider how you might make some changes for a more positive and welcoming morning routine. Observe what's working well and what you might like to change or shift. See if you can make three shifts in your routine by the end of the week.

WEEK 43

Music connects human beings. It brings people together. You can also describe it as energy: sound that moves air molecules. So a marching band will energize an athletic game or bring people to war. The bagpipe is used for war, for entertainment, for funerals, for weddings. Music is not one thing. It is something that people react to.

—YO-YO MA

Goal: Recognize the impact that music has on your body and mind. Use music intentionally to shift your emotional state.

Have you ever played a song with the intention to feel deeply? What songs might you put on to celebrate, to calm yourself, or to mourn?

Turn on the radio (in your home, car, or through the internet). Move through the music stations, listening to at least one minute of each station before finding the next. Observe: What are you looking for? How does the one minute of music make you feel? If the song feels great, why? How does the song match, lift, or conflict with your moods?

Try the same exercise with your music collection. Look through your collection to find something that fits with where you are at the moment. Play it and recognize the impact. Look again for an opportunity to use music to shift your mood when you want to intentionally change what you're feeling. There is an entire field of music therapy that uses music to shift emotional states. See if you can do this on your own.

TYPE: Social

Let us be grateful to people who make us happy; they are the charming gardeners who make our souls blossom.

—MARCEL PROUST

Goal: Identify a group that you are associated with and increase your participation, or seek out a group of people with whom you'd like to increase your involvement.

When you think about being part of a group, what comes to mind? Types of "groups" might include a music band, a company, a sports team, or a racial, cultural, or religious group. What kinds of groups do you consider yourself part of?

Continued >

During the COVID-19 pandemic, one of the most popular ways my clients engaged in intentional self-care was by forming groups. One client created a group for single professional women, and another created a spirituality group. My clients found that these groups were vital for their social and mental health during the pandemic. And even beyond such globally seismic moments, coming together as an intentional group can have profoundly beneficial effects.

In the prompt, you identified your groups. Do any stand out as a group with which you'd like to increase your involvement? How might you do that? Become a board member? Increase your participation? Get involved with advocacy work?

Are there groups that you're curious about? A choir, a bird-watching group, or a book club? In this week's entry or on a separate piece of paper, list five to ten groups that you might be interested in joining, or becoming more involved with.

WEEK 45

I am different from other people. People are different from me. We share a common humanity. I can learn from people who are different from me. And I can give them the gift of listening.

Goal: Engage with a person who is a very different age from you.

Who is the oldest person you know personally? The youngest? List some people at different phases on the age continuum from where you are (teenagers, grandparents, newlyweds, 20-somethings, babies, elementary school students, etc.).

Find one to three people who are at a different phase of life than you are. Ask them if they might have time to meet with you for a phone call, a cup of coffee, a video chat, or a meal. Let the person know that you're interested in their life and that you'd like to speak to them intentionally about their life, or even interview them.

Get to know this person on a more meaningful level. Ask open-ended questions about what matters to them, what they are proud of, and who their role models are. Find out how they spend their day, what they worry about, and what makes them laugh. Ask them about who they love, what they love to do, and what might be missing from their lives.

TYPE: Mental

I can encourage myself to do something that seems challenging. The encouragement I give myself will turn "I cannot" into "I have not yet." My self-talk is vital; the encouragement I give myself fosters my vitality.

Goal: Create new frameworks for encouraging, fostering, and facilitating your evolution and skill development. Recognize the importance of these frameworks for empowering your growth.

What do the words "respect," "trust," and "acceptance" mean to you? Please write thorough and thoughtful definitions for each of these terms.

Continued >

There is one parenting philosophy called RIE (Resources for Infant Educarers). The basic belief of RIE is that children can be respected, trusted, and accepted as the inventors, explorers, and self-learners they are.

Learning isn't just for children; adults learn too. This week, let's observe how we speak to ourselves about trying something new. Using the RIE approach, how do you trust and encourage yourself as a learner? How do you pursue your interests? Can you talk to yourself as you might talk with a child, encouraging them to try something new? Or do you hesitate and say, "I've never been good at X"? Observe the less encouraging words you may use with yourself.

Then, take stock of some activities you've thought about pursuing in the past. Painting? Activism? Running a race? Though you may feel as though the world at large has its own agenda for what you *should* do, what would you *like* to do?

As you consider these activities, notice if the negative voice returns. Hear the voice, but don't heed it. Continue to use the RIE method, and respect yourself as an inventor, explorer, and self-learner. If you lower the volume on the "You can't" voice, and amplify the RIE voice, what interests might you like to explore more deeply? List five in this week's entry, on a separate piece of paper, or in your own mind.

If you don't like something, change it; if you can't change it, change the way you think about it.

—MARY ENGELBREIT

Goal: Take stock of your life using the Whole Life Model (see page 141). Identify areas that are working really well and areas where improvement could be beneficial.

When you think of your *whole life*, what are the components that make up your life? What specific areas comprise your life (money, family, etc.), and how are they meaningful to you in different ways?

My favorite personal assessment tool is called the Whole Life Model, and I've modified it here with a distinct self-care focus. Give it a whirl! Consider the following five areas of your life as shown in this pie chart (along with some suggestions to frame how you think about each one):

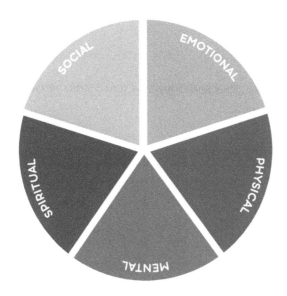

SOCIAL: Friends, Family

EMOTIONAL: Love & Partnership, Fun & Creativity

PHYSICAL: Physical Health, Environment

MENTAL: Finances, Career, Mental Health

SPIRITUAL: Volunteering, Personal Development, Spirituality

On a separate sheet of paper or in this week's entry, rank each area in terms of its *importance* to you on a scale of 1 (lowest) to 10 (highest). Rank again for how *satisfied* you are with this area of your life.

When you're done, subtract your satisfaction number from the importance number for each category. This is your "gap." The areas with the largest gaps are the ones you might want to prioritize for change. The ones with the smallest gaps can bolster you and help you through the change. Use this tool to reveal the strengths in your approach to self-care and the areas you might want to improve.

WEEK 48

You rest now. Rest for longer than you are used to resting. Make a stillness around you, a field of peace. Your best work, the best time of your life will grow out of this peace.

−PETER HELLER

Goal: Recognize the importance of short daily rest periods. Develop options for regular daily rests.

When was the last time you had a great rest? A nap in the middle of the day or zoning out on purpose in the sunlight? Recall when, where, and how you felt.

These days, many people are going hard all day every day. Thanks to omnipresent screens, our normal downtime (waiting on lines, waiting for a friend to arrive, daydreaming during a bus or train ride) has become catch-up time or stimulated time. We lack regular rest times throughout our day.

Brainstorm some options for rest. It can be active rest, like reading a book or meditating, or more passive rest, like taking a nap or just lying down. Other types of rest include stretching, yoga, sitting on a park bench, taking a long bath, or lying on the floor with your arms and legs stretched out as far as they can go.

Once you list a few, give yourself at least two intentional rest periods each day. If you use public transportation, use some of that time for rest. It can be as quick as a 10-minute rest or as long as a couple of hours. Just be sure to intentionally rest each day.

TYPE: Mental

And every day, the world will drag you by the hand, yelling, "This is important! And this is important!" . . . And each day, it's up to you to yank your hand back, put it on your heart, and say, "No. This is what's important."

—IAIN THOMAS

Goal: Take an inventory of your boundaries. Identify some boundaries that need reinforcement, or others that are fuzzy and could benefit from a clearer communication of boundaries. Identify some boundaries that are effective.

Can you remember the last time someone mentioned a boundary to you? Someone sharing that they are vegan or vegetarian or that they don't work weekends? How did you come to understand their boundary?

Continued >

Review some areas of your life where you are tolerating a situation that frustrates you. Some examples include: noisy neighbors, a coworker who repeatedly interrupts you, a close talker, or a friend who calls too early or shows up late consistently. List 20 of these "tolerances."

Now imagine that you are holding a magic wand. What would make each of these situations better?

Let's face it: Some of these situations are *not* going to improve. And some situations could benefit from a clearly established boundary, clearly communicated, such as a roommate who likes to get loud. Perhaps she can be as loud as she likes, just not after 10 p.m. or before 7 a.m. Or, you have a coworker who always interrupts. Make a little stop sign for your desk so she knows not to bother you when it's red and to proceed with caution when it's yellow.

Identify five boundaries you can set that will improve your life. Then set them.

I am impacted by scents. The scent of fresh-brewed coffee gives me one experience, and the smell of a newly mowed lawn gives me another. I can increase my awareness of the impact that different scents have on me.

Goal: Identify the value and impact of scents. Increase your opportunities to experience and enjoy scents. Add transformative scents to your life.

Is there a floral scent you love? A food scent? The smell of a person you care about? Think about scents that impact you—and why. Jot down a list of at least 10.

Smell. The best way to do this is with a series of short inhales through your nose. What do you smell? If your answer is nothing, keep going. Open the fridge, bring your clothes closer to your nose, and try again. What do you notice?

This week, smell something intentionally. Some of you may get down on the ground (*Go for it!*) and start smelling everything in your home, but others may be less thrilled with this exercise. Intentionally smell at least five things a day. That bowl of soup? Put your nose right into it, inhale, and let the scent wash over you. Your soap? Stop, sniff, and experience it. Snuggle in and smell the fur of a pet or the skin of someone you love. By the end of the week, you will have been thoughtful about experiencing 35 new smells. Keep a list in this week's entry or on a separate piece of paper, and keep going. Your nose is always with you. See how you can better enjoy this sense.

TYPE: Physical

I am held. When I lie down in the grass, the earth holds me. When I sit in the sun, the warmth embraces me. When I play music, the sound vibrations surround me. I am held.

Goal: Be held and hold someone else this week. Notice the impact of touch on your body and mind. Feel the difference between being held and holding.

What are your favorite textures? Cotton? Silk? Cashmere? Velour? Fleece? What are your favorite textures to hold against your skin?

Continued >

The impact of touch is significant. See if you can hold another living creature this week. A friend's dog or cat or bunny? Maybe you can go to a pet store and see if you can hold a hamster or a gecko. Animal shelters are often looking for people to hold dogs or cats. Touch helps these animals.

What is it like to hold another living being? To feel them yield in your arms? How does it make you feel?

Similarly, be held. Hold hands with a friend, or accept the embrace of another if that feels good to you. Float in a pool, or lie down in a hammock, bed, or couch. Observe what it is like to make contact with another living creature, and to be held by a person or by another life-form. How does it feel to yield, to relent, and to be held?

Between stimulus and response there is a space.
In that space is our power to choose our response.
In our response lies our growth and our freedom.

—VIKTOR E. FRANKL

Goal: Explore your range of response options in any given situation. Consider the concept of responding versus reacting.

Can you recall a time when you reacted to a situation and later regretted it? Perhaps you yelled at or overreacted to a store clerk, a friend, or a family member?

When we are met with a stimulus, we can react, or we can respond. A reaction happens so quickly, it can feel as if we're not in control of what is happening, but a response requires us to take a moment, think through our options, and choose the best one.

This week, your goal is to train yourself to respond, and *not* react. Recognize that in every situation, you can choose your attitude. Try to give yourself that extra beat each day in situations where you'd react, but a response might be more beneficial. Choose to take a moment each day, one where you might just have a knee-jerk reaction (like a car speeding by with its radio blaring or a child about to make a big old mess), and instead respond intentionally. Then observe. What happens to your lived experience after a week of thoughtful responses? Looking ahead, bring that thoughtfulness into your everyday.

Resources

VIA Institute on Character (Week 33)

To take a free survey to determine your top five character traits, visit VIACharacter.org. This self-assessment will take less than 15 minutes. If you want to pursue this further, there are also paid assessments that will dig deeper.

The Life-Changing Magic of Tidying Up: The Japanese Art of Decluttering and Organizing (Week 35)

Marie Kondo's best-selling book became an instant classic for two reasons: we want to have less mess and enjoy that which we have more. Her presentation style is delightful, and most find her gentle words to be unusually motivating. The cleaning almost takes care of itself because she shifts your mindset.

StoryCorps (Week 45)

If you are interested in learning more about interviewing the people in your life, visit StoryCorps.com. Their goal is to help build connection and compassion through storytelling. They provide tools and a story repository for everyone to enjoy.

Personal (R)evolution and the Whole Life Model (Week 47)

My book, Personal (R)evolution, is a nine-week, DIY coaching guide based on best practices with my clients. Chapter 2 is available for free on my website, AllisonTask.com, and gives you the full version of my Whole Life Model.

Calm

Calm is my favorite meditation app. In addition to "The Daily Calm," an ever-changing 10-minute daily meditation, the app provides sleep stories (for adults and kids), mini-courses, and music. They feature stories and meditation techniques from celebrities like Matthew McConaughey and Shaquille O'Neal.

Greater Good Science Center (GreaterGood.Berkeley.edu)

The University of California's web-based magazine's goal is to "bridge the gap between scientific journals and people's daily lives." With articles, videos, and quizzes, this site makes mental health easy to understand and actionable.

Dr. Kristin Neff and Self-Compassion (Self-Compassion.org)

If self-care involves action, self-compassion is a mindset. Dr. Kristin Neff is leading a movement to deliver more compassion to ourselves so that we can practice the habit of compassion and share it with the world.

The On Being Project (OnBeing.org)

This nonprofit media initiative, led by Krista Tippett, includes a public radio show, podcasts, and more. The goal is to "pursue deep thinking and moral imagination, social courage and joy, to renew inner life, outer life and life together."

References

Alcott, Jeanne. *Words of Power: 365 Inspirational Messages, Spiritual Powerlines, and Prayers.* WestBow Press, 2014.

Alcott, Louisa May. *Little Women.* Oxford University Press, 1994.

Angelou, Maya. *Rainbow in the Cloud: The Wisdom and Spirit of Maya Angelou.* Random House Publishing Group, 2014.

Barabási, Albert-László. *Bursts: The Hidden Patterns Behind Everything We Do, from Your E-Mail to Bloody Crusades.* Penguin Publishing Group, 2010.

Borges, Anna. *The More or Less Definitive Guide to Self-Care.* The Experiment, 2019.

Congdon, Lisa. *Whatever You Are, Be a Good One.* Chronicle Books, 2014.

Cowen, Alan S., and Dacher Keltner. "Self-Report Captures 27 Distinct Categories of Emotion Bridged by Continuous Gradients." *Proceedings of the National Academy of Sciences of the United States of America.* 114 (2017): E7900–09. DOI.org/10.1073/pnas.1702247114.

Flam, Jack D., ed. *Matisse on Art.* University of California Press, 1995.

Frankl, Viktor E. *Man's Search for Meaning.* Beacon Press, 2014.

Greater Good Science Center. "Three Good Things." GGIA.Berkeley.edu/practice/three-good-things.

Hay, Louise. *You Can Heal Your Life.* Hay House, 1984.

Hay, Louise. *I Can Do It: How to Use Affirmations to Change Your Life*. Hay House, 2004.

Hay, Louise. *Letters to Louise: The Answers Are within You*. Hay House, 2011.

Health Magazine. "Self-Care: The Ingredients for Health and Happiness." Special edition. January 2021.

Kondo, Marie. *The Life-Changing Magic of Tidying Up: The Japanese Art of Decluttering and Organizing*. Ten Speed Press, 2014.

Kotb, Hoda. *I Really Needed This Today: Words to Live By*. G. P. Putnam's Sons, 2019.

Lorde, Audre. *A Burst of Light and Other Essays*. Ixia Press, 2017.

Marchese, David. "Yo-Yo Ma and the Meaning of Life." *New York Times Magazine*, November 20, 2020. NYTimes.com/interactive/2020/11/23/magazine/yo-yo-ma-interview.html.

Milne, A. A. *Winnie-the-Pooh*. Penguin, 2009.

Nin, Anaïs. *Seduction of the Minotaur*. Swallow Press, 1961.

Obama, Michelle. *Becoming*. Crown Publishing Group, 2018.

Oprah.com. "Eating Green." April 22, 2009. Oprah.com/world/michael-pollan-omnivores-dilemma-environment-and-food/all.

Pollan, Michael. *Food Rules: An Eater's Manual*. Penguin Books, 2009.

Sherrow, Victoria. *Mohandas Gandhi: The Power of the Spirit*. Millbrook Press, 1994.

Venstra, Elizabeth. *True Genius: 1001 Quotes That Will Change Your Life*. Skyhorse Publishing, 2008.

Washington, Booker T. *Up from Slavery: An Autobiography*. Houghton Mifflin, 1928.

Williams, Nancy. *A Penny for Your Thoughts*. Readworthy Publications, 2009.

Wilson, Mel. "Our Most Valuable Non-Renewable Resource Is Time." *Huffington Post*. December 12, 2016. HuffingtonPost.ca/mel-wilson/sustainable-development-goals_b_13559152.html.

World Health Organization. "What Do We Mean by Self-Care?" Accessed June 4, 2021. WHO.int/reproductivehealth/self-care-interventions/definitions/en.

Yoga International. "Learning to Exhale: 2-to-1 Breathing." Accessed June 4, 2021. YogaInternational.com/article/view/learning-to-exhale-2-to-1-breathing.

ACKNOWLEDGMENTS

Aaron Task, thank you for taking care of our children during the pandemic so that I could write this book. Thank you for editing these words, and caring for our family and spirits. And for being my big crush.

Thank you, Matt Buonaguro, for finding me, and Jesse Aylen, Raluca Albu, and the team at Callisto for guiding me.

I thank every client who has given me the opportunity to work as a coach. It is a joy and privilege to serve you.

Thank you friends and clients who shared ideas and made this book better: Katya Lidsky, Cassidy Nasello, Cynthia Glidden, Grisel Pierrez, Cheryl Galante, Rachel Fishman Fedderson, Amy Azzarito, Lizzy Swick, Paul Regan, Lynn Walsh (and the Friday Morning Sisterhood), Aviva Patz, and Andy Rosenthal.

ABOUT THE AUTHOR

Allison Task, MS, PCC, works as a career and life coach. She has guided thousands of clients through significant life change over the last 20 years.

Allison is a sought-after coach, speaker, and thought leader. Prior to this book, Allison wrote *Personal (R)evolution, You Can Trust a Skinny Cook,* and *Lighten Up! America.* She hosted several television and internet shows, including Yahoo's Blue Ribbon Hunter, Lifetime's *Cook Yourself Thin,* and TLC's *Home Made Simple.*

Allison is a mother, partner, daughter, sister, ally, friend, neighbor, volunteer, colleague, and service dog owner. She splits her time between Montclair, New Jersey, and Lake Naomi, Pennsylvania.

CPSIA information can be obtained
at www.ICGtesting.com
Printed in the USA
JSHW020007180122
22049JS00003B/3